J. S. (Joseph Smith) Fletcher

Anima Christi

J. S. (Joseph Smith) Fletcher

Anima Christi

ISBN/EAN: 9783741173226

Manufactured in Europe, USA, Canada, Australia, Japa

Cover: Foto ©Andreas Hilbeck / pixelio.de

Manufactured and distributed by brebook publishing software (www.brebook.com)

J. S. (Joseph Smith) Fletcher

Anima Christi

DEDICATED

(BY PERMISSION)

TO

JOHN HENRY, CARDINAL NEWMAN,

IN TOKEN

OF UNDYING LOVE AND GRATITUDE.

Three years ago a small edition of Anima Christi was printed and circulated almost privately. As will be seen from the press opinions given at the end of this book it was received with praise—more praise, the author fears, than in its then shape the work merited. Since that time he has seen many faults in his poem, and from time to time has made alterations and corrections in it. He now republishes it in a complete form. He is only too conscious of its imperfections, and no one will see its faults more clearly than himself. There can be no greater theme in this age than the one he has chosen, nor yet one more difficult of adequate treatment.

ANIMA CHRISTI.

PART ONE.

A man forsakes God and is desolate.

I.

I believe in nothing whatever, for life is a sham and a lie.—
Life with its wonderful shiftings and ceaseless changes of scene,
Which has come to me unasked, and is passing me quickly by,
So quickly that soon 't will have gone altogether, and I shall have been.

And I know not if 'tis worth living, but live
  it I will and must.
 Where it will lead to I know not, nor care,
  but one thing I know,—
There is no such thing as a God, be He cruel
  and faithless, or just;
 Nor is there eternal gladness or never
  ending woe.

A God! O mad, fond blindness that men
  should be such fools
 As to dream of something better than what
  themselves they are!
Away with all their precepts and the learning
  of their schools
 And their dogmatised theology imported
  from afar.

Gods and religions and systems—there must
  be a thousand or more,
 If each God-believing sect is, as it thinks it
  is, quite in the right.

List to them now, just listen, how they bellow
    and wrangle and roar,
  And keep up their wordy mouthings through
    day and through eve and night.

Which of them has it? Why none: they are
    all of them liars and knaves,
  All preaching and praying for gold, and
    hugging themselves in fear
Of their lucre slipping away, ah yes, they are
    thorough slaves
  To their own base motives, keep off them,
    and go not near.

For their fever is highly infectious and might
    seize one. But which of the lot
  Should one take as a prophet where each
    thinks the other is wrong?
For one says his is the true faith, and another
    bawls out it is not,
  And the noise is more than confusing, yet
    somehow they all jog along.

And papist elbows protestant, and shows him
    the stake and the fire,
  And grinds in his unwilling ears a babble
    of barbarous words;
And moving his puppet-like flocks by some
    invisible wire
  He sets them to wipe out sin by means of
    armies and swords.

And one like a clown in a circus tricks him
    out with dresses and gauds,
  And lights his candles before him and offers
    up the host,
While another preaches him down with blatant
    hurrying words;
  And two more wrangle yonder about the
    Holy Ghost.

And one says Christ was God, and another
    says Nay, 'tis not so;
  And a creature there says the Spirit came
    both from Father and Son,

While his neighbour laughs him to scorn as
    though himself should know,
And proceeds to explain very wisely that it
    only proceeded from one.

And each is wrangling and wrangling and
    struggling along in the fight
Of sects and systems and churches, and tells
    you with countenance bold,
That he, as others are wrong, is surely in the
    right,
And that there only is One Shepherd and
    that he has but One Fold!

II.

No, I will have no dealing with these
They may wear out their horny knees
Ere ever I pray to their God to help me!
How can a God Who is served in so many ways
Be worthy of praise?
That I cannot see.
They would doubtless tell me a so-called truth
Out of that strange old book
Their Bible, in which I never look
Except to read a simple story
Which for me is possest of a wondrous glory,
And which you will find in the book of Ruth.

For I remember, perhaps too well,
How my mother was wont to tell,
Long years since in the happy hours
Of childhood, that amidst the flowers
And golden stubble, beneath the bright
Eastern skies with their burning light,
Ruth went gleaning in Boaz' sight.
I remember, as though 'twere yesterday,
When my sister and I were tired of play,
How she would call us to her knee
And tell us of Ruth, and bid us be
Like her, obedient, good and kind.
—And now she is dead and lies enshrined
Down there in the aisle of the little church
Where she used to make such wondrous search
After this God that they preach of and pray to,
For she went and prayed there thrice-a-day.
If anyone knows it, she knew the way to
That heaven one dreams of once in a way.

And when I was a child I used to go
With her to the little church below
In the valley, and listen to what was said
By the surpliced and stoled one overhead,

Who was high in his doctrine, and preached
    ex-tempore,
And said he could show us the way to glory,
Though he ended by nearly going to jail.
For he and his bishop could never get on,
And the parson would have wax-candles upon
His holy altar and thurify it
With incense, perhaps to purify it.
His reading ended with a wail
Of intonation ; his singing choir
Who sang while he took time to respire
Where clothed in short bed-gowns white as
    snow,
With a long, black, high-necked garment below,
While he himself was wrapped and covered
In copes and albs. He scraped and bowed
When he stood at the altar as though there
    hovered
Some wonderful being in the incense-cloud.
And he would'nt say some of the prayers aloud;
And he preached real presence and called
    confession
A means of grace, and said that when death
Took away from the body its life and breath,

ANIMA CHRISTI.   9

The soul didn't go straight off to heaven,
But was helped to get there by intercession.
And news of all this to the bishop was given,
Who being low church, and prosy, and old,
And thoroughly protestant, very soon told
This zealous priest, his christian brother
Most dearly beloved, to seek out another
Sphere of work or to drop such preaching,
For he would have no catholic teaching
Nor catholic service within his realm.
But this didn't seem to overwhelm
The parson, whose people defended him,
So at length the bishop, in sorrow and tears,
Gave him a holiday for two years,
Or, in other words, suspended him.
  Yet it did no good his being away,
For his curates did things the very same way,
And even added some details more
In the matter of dresses and candles,—and when
The parson came back to his church again,
All went on as it did before.

But as an outsider, I never could see
What sort of a system that might be

Which gave one man who, as I knew,
Was a very worldly old being, the power
To tell another who was as true
And courteous a one, though spoiled by the blind
Belief in God which lived in his mind,—
That he only should preach when he, his lord
In spiritual power, should give him the word.
But of course it was one of the christian laws
Of brotherly love. I remember now
How the bishop and parson once had a row—
A wordy argument, all because
The latter would preach in a coloured stole!
—Now what could *that* have to do with the soul?

III.

Well, let them wrangle and fight:
They and their God can make it up at last,
I will have none of them, for I know
When they say there is God that it is not so.
The days of God and religion are past!
The world is waking all over to own the great
    being, Man!
Is man a thing so weak or slight
As to have to trust on a God whom he cannot
    see?
I would sooner the whole race ran
And pressed its native earth with bended knee
To a God of wood or copper or stone,
Than that it should trust on a God whom it
    sees by faith alone.

IV.

God was well enough in the days of primeval
  earth,
 He fitted in with the customs and suited
  the savage times,
For they sacrificed babes to Him then which
  had only just known birth
 In the hope that the blood-loving being
  would smile on their murd'rous climes.

We are nothing better now for men trust what
  they do not see,
 And look to another world when they shall
  have lost their breath
And taken their leave of this one. So think
  they, but as for me,
 I know there is no hereafter and that death
  is an endless death.

Heaven and hell? There is neither, and there
   certainly is no God
 To will man away to either. Ah, well, let
   them rest in their faith
In this wondrously mixed-up something who
   can damn them by his nod;
 This God and his religion of phantom and
   of wraith.

I will have none of either: I believe in nothing
   at all.
 I look on all that is with a quite indifferent
   mind;
I hate all priestcraft and praying as though
   they were bitterest gall;
 I am a law to myself in myself, and I throw
   all else to the wind.

V.

I have just been down to the village in the
    dusk of the dying day,
  And heard a labourer talking of me at his
    cottage door,
And without a thought of mischief I listened
    to what he might say,
  Hearing no good of myself, as a fool could
    have told me before.

'I be puzzled with Squoire, I be; he be naught
    of a man, sure-ly;
  Don't believe in a God or a heaven, nor even
    a hell!
And say there aint no more o' you arter you
    die,
  But he aint convinced me its right, and I
    don't think he's sartin himsel'!

'For he allus looks moody, does Squoire,
 a-poking and podging about,
And reading big books all day, and watching
 the stars o' nights;
With his face an' hands as smooth and white
 as a new-washed clout,
And his eyes as burning and bright as the
 parson's altar lights.

'Parson and squoire don't mix, as it isn't
 likely they should
When one on 'em says there's a God and the
 other 'un says there aint.
An' it allus comes out in th' nursin' what's
 been grafted i' th' blood,
An' we all on us knows that *old* squoire
 were not by no means a saint!

'I don't 'old noways wi' parson, wi' his dresses
 and incense that smells;
Tho' I weänt say he doesn't do good; for
 he's powerful kind to the poor,

But I don't agree with his sarvice, nor the
    singin' that's like dog's yells,
  An' me and my missis is members at the
    Methodis' chapel next door.

'And Pogson he preached last night about
    'ternal life and death,
  And he spoke of the fearful torments that
    summun would undergo
As didn't believe in a God; And sister Snigsby,
    she saith,
  That Pogson meant the Squoire, as she
    'appened pertikler to know!'

VI.

Last night I dreamt a vision came and said
That I should not be happy while I kept
These dark dim notions in my head:
And then it went; and when again I slept,
My sister, golden-haired and azure-eyed,
Who died too young came to my side
Dressed in pure white and crowned with stars
Of perfect light and bade me see
What there was kept in store for me.
She passed away: I woke. Between
The oriel window's oaken bars,
The moon looked in with calm, clear light,
Lighting the spot where she had been.
And lying sleepless through the night
I wondered what it all might mean.

I cannot forget that dream.
Why did my mother and sister come, and from
 where?
Can it be that there,
Wherever they are, they can see
What is happening to me?
Howe'er it is so it would seem.
But then, fool that I am—it is matter for
 laughter,—
How can they know who are dead when there
 is no hereafter?

VII.

I have no cause to be sad:
I have all that can please man's heart.
Horses and hounds and money and land,
And all that is good to see,
And yet I am never glad,
But feel as though the brand
Of despair were stamped on the part
Where I fancy my brain to be.

VIII.

Nine years ago to-day
I saw them lay her body in the earth—
My little sister, who from birth
Was ever with me in work or play.
Nine years ago, nine years to-day.
How fair she looked, her face did seem
As though she lay but in a dream,
Yet she was dead and gone. Gone where?
Can it be true that something is there
In the hereafter whereof she
Has solved the eternal mystery,
And that a halo of heavenly grace
Circles around her golden head?
I do not like to think her dead
For ever, for her calm still face
Wore a bright smile which seemed to say
That life was not all taken away,
That she was not of all bereft
But that an inner life was left
And gone to some more perfect day.

IX.

I am half in doubt of my creed.
—Life is worth living indeed,
If it but the prelude is
To some state of rest and bliss,
But if there is nothing to come after death;
If there be no other life than this,
I begin to think it were best to have done with breath.

X.

I know not where I came across this doubt
That haunts me, mocking at my Godless faith,
And whispering that my creed is but a wraith
Of miserable phantoms, devil-sown,
Breeding sad thought and endless misery,
And likening it to one prolongèd groan,
But where or whatever it be
I will somehow fathom it out.

XI.

I am more and more opprest
By doubts and wonders and fears,
And I went last night to a chest
Which I have not opened for years,
And, not without some tears
Took from its dust-covered rest
A little Testament bound in red,
Which belonged to my sister who is dead;
And all through the night in the gloom
Of what was once her room
I sat with a single light and read
Of the life of Him who is called the church's
    head
And of His death and doom.

And, believing nothing, I still could see
Something within this history
Which looked like truth even unto me;
Till I began to wonder and wonder
However so strange a mystery
As a God who is one and one in three,
And Who is always and ever asunder,
And yet one person can anyway be.

XII.

I am thoroughly wretched and sad
Is the creed I have clung to wrong?
Is there a God, is there another world?
Is there a heaven? Is there a hell
Where the damned will be suddenly hurled
To live in fire for long
Years of fierce torment? Ah well,
If I do not somehow these doubts dispel
I shall go mad!

XIII.

Ah, tell me, some one, tell me if it all be a
sham and a lie,
This thing that is borne upon me by some
invisible power,
Which steals on my heart and my brain when
no other being is nigh,
Watching for ever by me and whispering,
every hour,

With cruel insidious tongue, strange fancies
that make me afraid;
Fancies that tell me my life has been
nothing but sorrow and sin,
Spent in the dark, dread presence of a devil
who casts his deep shade
Over the life of all to whom he enters in.

I am in shadow enough: but where is the
    light?
  Where is the star of hope? Where is the
    sun of my day?
Where is there one to guide me out of this
    awful night
  Where I roam with never a being to whom
    I can look or pray?

Is there nothing in life to live for, nothing to
    do or to be?
  Must I always be steeped in these fancies,
    ever tormented with fear?
Is there none in this vast world to come and
    be with me
  And bear with my sin and my sorrow, and
    hold me a little dear?

XIV.

O lost in the black abysses of this damnèd
　　dark despair,
Where shall my heart find rest? Tell me, O
　　tell me, where!

PART TWO.

For awhile he finds rest in human love.

I.

What is it that shall wake
 The fulness of the life that in me lies?
What is it that shall break
 The long, long spell which now shuts close
  mine eyes?
What is it that shall come
 And lift me out of all that I am now,
Out of the tired world's weary whirl and hum,
 And change the dreaming thoughts that
  haunt my brow
Into fierce streams of life that quick shall soar
 Away from earth and so to heights above,
And make me what I ne'er have been before?
 Tell me if it be Love.

What is it? O mother of all,
 Fair Nature that hath ever seemed more sweet

Than any music that did ever fall
  Upon my ears, about whose jewelled feet
I as a child have played—
  Tell me, fair monitress, what subtle change,
What wondrous transformation must be made
  Ere I who from my very birth did range
In all that the world holds good, shall know
    thee far
  Fairer than ever, and more subtly move
Through worlds of light that undiscovered are?
  Tell me if it be Love.

What is it? And what is this
  Which we call Love and which I do not know?
Is it a simple kiss,
  A pressing of heart to heart, a hurrying flow
Of passionate phrase and speech,
  Of sweet indefinite longing that makes way
Into the very core of life, until it reach
  The glad, grand point when all is swept away
Of forces that oppose or that conspire
  To bar its path? Sweet stars that shine above
Tell me from whence ye catch your sacred fire—
  Is it from Love?

II.

I have seen her again to-day.
An hour ago in the little church there on the
    hill
I was ling'ring, absorbed in the flood
Of various-tinted light which poured on the
    spot where I stood
From the eastern window, and suddenly coming
    my way
A step; and I turned, and it seemed that my
    heart grew still.

For she stood there; she.
Never till yesterday
Had I seen her; but yesterday in a sudden
    glance
I saw her, and knew that in all this earth, to me
No woman could ever be fairer than this.
Ah, will it ever be that it shall be my bliss
To hold her within my arms and with passionate
    kiss
Know her my own?

Never till yesterday
Had I seen her, and yet she already is grown
So dear that my heart has longed since yesterday
To make her my love, my queen, my very own!

And even now I know not
If she be maiden or wife.
So strange are the freaks of love that a lover
Waits no hour to discover
Aught of his love. A wife? I trow not.
She is too young, and the innocent maiden-life
Looks out from the blue of her eyes and seems
    to speak
To a would-be lover in accents such as these
*If thou wouldst gain my love or in any way
    please,*
*Thy heart must be made as pure as the heart
    thou dost seek.*

It is good that it should be so.
A love that does not ennoble 's of little worth.
I would have a love that should lift me out of
    the earth

And create a heaven about me of all things good
And uncommon, wherein I might breathe a
 diviner air
And learn many sacred things which before I
 did not know.
It seemed to day as I stood
And watched her, that everywhere
The world was grown more fair
And that life made promise that all should be
 fairer far
Because of the rising of Love, the morning star.

Well, and however it be,
Whether she will love me,
Or whether her heart already is given away,
Her lover am I for ever since yesterday.
So lacking of patience am I in the office of lover
That I will not tarry one hour to discover
If she be free.
I will go on in the path which is opened
 before me.
— And here are the linnets singing, to re-
 assure me,—
She is for thee—for thee—for thee!

III.

I have found my rest.
The shapeless phantoms of my fevered brain
Are past, are gone, are vanished with the night.
O heart, rejoice; they will not come again!
The future lies before thee, clear and white,
The future, filled with happy, happy light,
The future, a bright island of the blest.

I have found my rest.
The doubts that dwelt within my mind of yore
Are fled far off to some black gulf of hell.
O mind, rejoice; they will not haunt thee more!
The future lies before thee, promising well,
Like some long stream whose course no man
    may tell,
But which looks fair to him that takes the quest.

I have found my rest.
The night is gone, the clouds are passed away,
And there is risen above my head the star
Of Love, dear Love, who took me from the fray
To battle for him in his own sweet war
Of whispered words and glances that words are;
Wise Love, who knows that love for man is best.

I have found my rest.
The arms of Love are round me evermore,
The voice of Love is in my ear alway.
O golden sun, that from the Eastern shore
Castest a path of light across the bay,
Rise higher, higher! Is not this the day
When I shall take my love unto my breast?

I have found my rest.
O sun-lit morning, look upon her now!
O breath of flower and foliage steal to her!
O sunlight, touch the blossoms at her brow;
O Love, be with her wheresoe'er she stir,
For she is all thine own, thy minister,
Whom thou with thine own loveliness hast blest.

I have found my rest.
O bridal day, be glad, be fair, be bright!
O time fly on with love's untrammelled feet
Through happy day to happy, happier night,
And bring me to my own, my love, my sweet,
That all our being in one long kiss may meet,
And I may hear her maiden love confest.

IV.

As one who wanders cheerless and forlorn
Through darkened paths ere yet the sun be risen:
As one who lies within some loathsome prison
Watching with hungry eyes for signs of morn:
Even as either sees at length the dawn
And cries aloud, clapping his hands in glee:
So did I look for, so do I look on thee.

As one that drifts across a harbour bar,—
Going out unhelmed beneath the hurrying breeze:
As one who voyages 'mid unknown seas
Uncompassed, where all manners of peril are:
Even as either sees at last a star
Shine from the heavens with friendly brilliancy,
So did I look for, so do I look on thee.

V.

O best of All,
O mighty influence that will never die,
O strange sweet passion, as the summer sky
Cloudless and pure! Whatever men thee call,
Still art thou, Love, the same.
What though we know not thee, nor even thy
    name,
We feel thy might, thy mystery, and we
Turn from ourselves to thee,
O Love, the power that shall for ever be.

ANIMA CHRISTI.

We know not what thou art:
And yet we feel that thou art Lord and King
Of all that dwells within the human heart.
O pleasant time, O gladness of the spring,
When thou O Love with quick invisible wing
Lit on my brow and said to care, Depart
And be at peace, and thou, rest from the smart
Of lovelessness, henceforward thou art mine,
Mine ever, mine alone.   O Love divine,
O springtime, O sweet madness of the earth;
To wake to love is as a new bright birth!
Is this the world that once I thought so dark,
Or that the sky which once I found so drear?
Are these the woods I cared not for? But hark:
Bells, from the village belfry old and grey,
Fling happy sound across the wooded park,
Startling the deer that wander there away,
Waking the echoes of the ruins here,
And telling me it is my marriage day.
White day of all the whitest days of spring!
O happy bells, ring on, for ever ring;
It is my marriage day!

VI.

Where the still sunlit garden reposes,
   Shut in from the rest of the land
By woods and by streams and by closes,
   Which stretch to the wave-washed strand
   Of shingle and rock and brown sand,
     In front of the white-breastèd sea,
There are thousands and thousands of roses,
   But never a rose like thee.

I have read in some old Eastern story,
   Some legend of long years ago,
Of a flower that was clothed with all glory,
   A flower that had petals of snow:
   And the flower of the legend I know
     Was fair as a fair flower can be;
But no flower of legend or story
   Is like unto thee!

VII.

A light on the cliffs by the sea?—
Nay it is only a star that peeps over the hill,
A star that came out from the heavens of its own sweet will,
And is wandering slowly across the deserted shore
To gaze for awhile on thee,
And to see itself eclipsed and its brightness made poor
By the light of the eyes that are brighter than stars to me.

There is no light like the light of the eyes
    that I love;
Not all the stars that are there in the heaven
    above,
Not all the myriad lights that glimmer and
    glance on the sea,
Are bright as the eyes which will smile upon
    mine alway;
Not even the cloudless skies of a sunny day
Are bright as the dear blue eyes which shall be
My stars for ever and aye.

Love who is Lord over all hath made his decree
And bade me to serve in his courts not by year
    nor by day,
But for ever and ever, and I will obey his behest.
Love who is Lord over all, does he not know
    best
What is best for us all? So for ever and ever
I will love thee and thou me, and we two will
    part never!

VIII.

What if this life shall not go on for ever,
What though there be no other world than this,
What if the grave be our sole end and aim?
Even then our life of love will be the same.
That shall not spoil our three-days-wedded bliss.
Ah, little one, why will you thus endeavour
To show me that I am indeed to blame
In daring to deny your God, why wonder
That I believe in nothing, and why ponder,
O sweetest preacher, with those downcast eyes,
On the hard fact that I who am so wise

In your opinion should refuse to see
That there is aught amiss or wrong in me,
Because I do not choose the creed to say,
Because I will not kneel down twice-a-day
As you in your sweet innocent whiteness do?
Well, never mind.—See, I will pray to you,
And you shall grant me everything I ask,
And bid me do whate'er you wish; the task
Will be sweet Love's, and he is now my God.
Am I not ready to obey each nod,
Each rule of his? He is the God for me,
You his high-priest!

IX.

Ah, let me never wake
If this be but a dream,
If this sweet hand which in my own I take
Be not what it seem;
If the clear lovelit gleam
Of those dear eyes be but a fancy, brought
From out a fevered brain,
From out a mind o'erwrought,
Let me not wake, let me not live again!

Let me sleep on for aye.
Yes, let me dream that I have once been loved,
Have known for once a perfect cloudless day
In the dark winter of this life, and moved
Once through bright paths o'er which no
    shadow lay.
If this be but a sleep,
O let me sleep for ever and for ever!
O let me dream that once mine eyes did weep
Warm tears of love and gladness; let me know,
If but in sleep, of love the passionate flow
And sudden joy. O if this should be so,
Let me wake never!

X.

Yes, and indeed this love of mine shall be
A very God, a very lord to me.
O thou unknown and fabled deity,
Whom some, by superstitious fear made blind,
Profess to find in every breath of wind,
In every blade of grass, in every flower;
If thou indeed dost live, if there is *thee*
In aught about me, show it me this hour!
Show me, thou God, if God thou art, thy power,
See, how I mock thee! Nay, but thou art not.
See how I scorn thee! Let it not be forgot.
God? O pale myth, thou art not, shalt not be:
Keep thine own place, man hath no need of
    thee,
No need, no need, O fabled one!

But see,
For I would dare thee aught whom I not know,
If thou art God, prove it that thou art so.
If thou art God show me thy power, God, show.
Need'st thou some means? Then, if a God
    thou be
Snatch from my life what is most dear to me!

    *   *   *   *   *

I know not if I wake, or if I sleep,
But if I sleep, I dream.—O let me wake!
Begone, ye damnèd shapes, begone, I say!
God, if there be a God, cast them away!
See, how they drag me downward to the deep;
See, how they mock my agony and creep
Into my brain and heart and life, and make
All things another Hell. O let me die.
Save me O save me!
                    There is some one by.
What is it night, and do I dream? Have I
Been sleeping long or am I ill? And why
Do you all speak in whispers? Who is this,
And where is?—

ANIMA CHRISTI.

     O like a flash of light I know!
I know it all; 'tis burnt upon my brain,
'Tis stamped upon my heart and in my life.
O let me die! She cannot come again:
Did I not see her *dead?*
         O the black woe!
Five days, but five short days of Spring my wife,
And gone.
     See, she is there, is there.
Ah, darling, take me to thee!—What, you too,
My sister, with your long, bright golden hair,
Radiant in stars—both fair as when I knew
You both and kissed you. Ah, stay by me now,
Sister and wife.
     Nay, see upon my brow
Sits a black devil; touch me not, but flee!
—Ah God, I pray Thee, take my life from me!

XI.

Ah God, from off my brain
Take this black curse, this fierce undying pain,
Take it away! I own Thee: Thou art God!
God, by the strength of Thy Almighty power,
God, by the weight of Thy chastising rod,
God, by the prayers that seek Thee ev'ry hour,
Why hast Thou taken all I loved from me?
God, Thou art God, and Thou hast won.
    Yet see,
O being of power and pride and cruelty,
I own Thee God, but I will serve Thee never:
God, wheresoe'er Thou art, whate'er Thou be
Thee I reject for ever and for ever!

PART THREE.

He is once more desolate.

I.

I am alone; alone in a world that is but a
    fleeting show,
  A world which has proved so vile that I
    should not in it linger
If I had but the pluck of a man. God! it
    were easy to go!
  Here is the very thing to do it with. The
    pull of a finger

Would send this bit of lead through my brain
    with a smash and a crash.
  How easy it were to do it and get away
    from the light!

Here goes.—But when did I ever do anything
 wild or rash;
　I will think it over once more, and besides
 —that vision last night.

Vision of wife and mother and sister robed in
 white,
　Star-crowned and carrying palms and smiling
 all on me,
And a whisper which seemed to say, In the
 land of endless light
　We are waiting, O thou whom we love,
 waiting to welcome thee!

In the land of endless light? Where is it?
 Thou God whom I hate,
　Thou despot that snatched away my five-
 days'-bride from me;
Dost thou in Thy mighty mind, which Thy
 followers teach is great,
　Know where in space or creation any such
 land may be?

II.

I will go down to the church and stand by her
    grave awhile.
'Tis eighteen months to-day since she gave me
    her last sweet smile
And went to swift death! Why went she?
              Ah wife with the soul so white,
I would give—what would I not give to be
    where thou art to-night!

III.

O'er the soft brown autumn meadows steals
    the last light of the sun,
Falling softly, shortening quickly, telling me
    that day is done;
Telling me that day is over, gone another day
    from me,
O my darling, let it perish if it brings me
    nearer thee!

Roses blossom o'er thy bosom, O my rose I
    see not now,
Lilies white are lying o'er thee, not so white
    as was thy brow,

Flowers have sprung to life above thee where thou liest still and dead,
With the cross which thou so lovedst standing silent at thy head.

O my wife, my love, my lost one, would that thou wert here with me!
Would that I might draw thee to me with the hand I gave to thee,
Would that thou couldst teach me patience, would that thou mightst take my hand
In thine own and lead me onward to some far-off mystic land.

Where is never sin or sorrow, where is neither fear nor shame,
Where no crowd of mortals hurries after unenduring fame,
Where the light is clear and cloudless as the twilight heaven above,
Where is nought of hate or sadness, where is rest and peace and love.

I have sinned; none knows it better, and my
    heart would fain have rest.
O that I could clasp thee to me, hide my
    sorrows in thy breast,
Feel thy lips upon my forehead, and thy hand
    within my own,
And thy heart pressed close to my heart ere it
    harden into stone!

Vain regrets! for thou hast left me. Shall I
    ever see thee more?
Wilt thou meet me when my foot falls on that
    distant unknown shore
Which is lying undiscovered, which my feet
    have never trod,
Where thy spirit is for ever? But I have no
    faith in God.

I am proud and I would scorn Him, I would
    curse Him, I would be
Cursed and outcast for all ages if it had not
    been for thee;

But thou lovedst Him; were He worthy of
    such priceless love as thine
I would love Him too, and fear Him, and
    would hail Him all-divine.

Ah, my lost one, if thou hearest, keep me with
    thy strongest prayer!—
Fool, I know not what I ask for, none hath
    ever listened there.
Had a wish of man e'er echoed in those
    spaceless halls on high,
Christ, the one propitiation, would have had
    no need to die.

No, there is no use in praying, yet I would
    that thou couldst hear,
That thy voice could speak in whispers, that
    thy presence might be near.
There is left in earth no comfort, there remains
    no peace for me
Who have known a very heaven in the love
    that was of thee.

O but I am wretched truly, and my mind with
    vague unrest
Tears my heart in myriad pieces; would that
    I might find some rest!
Now that thou art taken from me what have
    I to do with life?
Would to God that I were buried in this grave
    with thee my wife!

IV.

Long years are gone
And still I live who have not strength to die.
I know not how the weeks and months pass by.
Would that that day might have its being
    when I
Shall look my last upon
The world and end my life of misery.

There are whose hearts are filled
With sorrow till the strings do almost break.
—O God if Thou art skilled
To heal such wounds, heal mine; and from
    me take
The darkness and despair which Thou hast
    willed
That I should bear and I have born long years:
For her dear sake for whom I shed these tears,
Whose love through all my life and being
    thrilled,
For her dear sake!

V.

I passed to-day at noontide through the little
    Italian town
  Where my feet have lingered so long because
    of the sunny skies,
And remembered that in England the leaves
    are turning brown.
  Shall I go back to-morrow? Shall I—will
    it be wise?

My steps would tend to the spot which I see
    wherever I go!
  That little white cross and the roses and
    lilies around
Are always present with me in land of sunlight
    or snow,—
  I can always call up to mem'ry the tiny
    churchyard mound.

There my love lies dead and silent, and there
    my life has lain
  Years and years in dull torment till its
    feelings are almost flown
Because of the never-ending and ever-wearing
    pain
  That had done me no greater evil had it
    turned my heart to stone.

VI.

Another spring and still I linger here,
And why I know not. Every day I see
And hear of things which are unwise to me.
I see the peasant bow his head and pray
To senseless stone, and this idolatry
Would surely send me shuddering away
But that of late a subtle sense of fear
Across my heart has placed its sterner sway,
And bade me linger till my life is clear.

VII.

Here is the church: the peasants crowd the
    way.
'What is the matter, good woman?'
                                  'Sir, to-day
'It is the Corpus Christi and we go
'To hear the mass; and after that, you know,
'One of the Franciscans is to preach.'
                               —Some monk
Who loves the grape far better than God's love,
The cellar than the mystic heaven above,
And fasting not so well as to be drunk!
I will go in and look at him—.

VIII.

The words are ringing yet within my ears—
'Is any weary? I will bear him up.'
Strange words—strange power. In all my life
    before,
Through all the darkness of the buried years
—Buried but not forgotten—such strong will
Ne'er conquered mine. Have I not drained
    the cup
Of sorrow and despair and bitterness
Unto its dregs, and longed to reach some shore
Where peace reigns and there are not any tears.

He spoke, that pale dark friar, as if his mind
Dwelt at most perfect peace; as though he knew
The truth of what he said. The keen words flew
From out his lips like wingèd barbs and I
Felt all their force. And have I then been blind
Even as the fool wrapped up in the thick cloak
Of his own empty reasoning? O why
Did I go there and break that easy yoke
Which held my soul, my heart till yesterday?
I know not what it is to kneel or pray:
I have no love, or had not—have I now?—
For aught that is, and yet those swift words woke
Some chord that slept within me, and my brow
Seemed eased of the black load that on it lay.

O wife, if thou art list'ning to me now
Aid me! Mad prayer—the dead can hear no more.
Her spirit, if indeed on some far shore
It lives and moves, can hold no speech with mine,

Nor listen to my restless pleadings. How
Or whence shall I find guidance, whence divine
The truth that seems to steal mysteriously
With subtle promptings softly over me?

To-night, as the sun set beyond the sea
I lingered by the way. The Angelus
Came floating o'er the meadows to my ears;
A peasant who was lingering near to me
Dropped on his knees: the low-breathed words
    I caught—
'Mother of God, sweet Mary, pray for us
Now and when death is nigh.' Why did the
    tears
Start to my eyes at hearing words so fraught
With superstition and idolatry?
I cannot tell: I know not where I go
Nor whither I am led: I cannot pray
Because I have no God, and yet I feel,
—Or is it only madness tells me so?
That I am blindly brought along some way
And taught strange things that make my heart
    to glow
And newer visions through my life to steal.

IX.

*The Franciscan Monastery.   Midnight.
     A monk praying.*

'Lord, by Thine Agony and Bloody Sweat,
Lord, by Thy Strife and Anguish on the Tree,
If there be any soul that doth regret
Its life of sin, O turn it unto Thee!
Thou canst do all things Who in fight hast met
The power of sin and gained the victory.'

PART FOUR.

He looks back over his past life.

I.

I know Thee now! Ah let me stay for ever
  Here at Thy side, O cast me not away!
Here let me stay, here let me make endeavour
  To kiss Thy feet and serve Thee day by day.

I have known sin. Who is there of the living
  That e'er hath plunged to those black gulfs
    of hell
From which Thy hand hath drawn me, all
    forgiving?
Nay, there is none that can fall as I fell.

And now I know Thee. Like some wondrous
    vision
  Thou, Soul of Christ, didst come unto my
    heart.
Wilt Thou not stay and save me from perdition,
  Ah, most sweet Lord, say Thou wilt not
    depart!

Here is my heart; it is no house of glory,
  It hath no roof upreared to touch the sky,
Nor window blazing with a dead saint's story,
  Nor vaulted dome, nor altar rising high.

Nor hath it aught of brightness in its keeping:
  It is but flesh, and it is dark with sin,
And myriad faults within its gloom lie sleeping,
  But O Lord Christ wilt Thou not enter in?

Enter, and I will bless Thy name for ever!
  I know Thee now; I, who did once blaspheme
Thy Holy Name and swore to serve Thee never,
  Have started up affrighted from my dream,

To find Thee watching o'er my sore affliction.
  Was that the way by which Thou brought'st
    me home?
Ah blessèd Lord, mine is most true conviction,
  Take Thou my hand, nor let me further roam.

O how I love Thee who for ever blessèd
  Will cling to Thee and at Thy altar kneel!
But when wilt Thou have half Thy love
    confessèd
  O Soul of Christ that meltest hearts of steel?

I have seen all that earth can show of sorrow,
  I have known all that man can know of love,
Kissed lips that promised kisses for to-morrow,
  Looked into eyes that shone like stars above:

Clasped hands which trembled with the heart's
    emotion,
  Smiled back on smiles which tender thoughts
    confest,

Whispered warm words that told of true devotion,
    Stood tranced from life and strained to woman's breast:

I have known all; and O, how vastly higher
    How much more wondrous is Thy love, O Christ,
For those whom Thou hast snatched from out the fire,
    For those for whom Thyself was sacrificed.

There is no love of father or of mother,
    There is no love of maiden or of wife,
There is no love of sister or of brother,
    There is no love that lives in any life,

Such as the love wherewith, O thou All-saving,
    Thou hast loved me who am not fit to live;
Didst Thou not die, and, all things calmly braving,
    Come unto me, my black sins to forgive.

O how Thou lov'st me! never earthly passion
 Was half so strong as is this love of Thine !
Was ever love that loved in this sweet fashion,
 Was ever heart that woke such love in mine?

I will stay here, O love and Lord, for ever,
 Kissing Thy feet and serving Thee alway;
I will be Thine and wander from Thee never,
 Until the shadows pass from me away.

II.

But once I knew, nor shall I soon forget it,
  That shape of shame which haunts the mind
    .   of man,
Yea, once I knew, and with glad welcome met it,
  Or towards its shadow with quick longing ran.

Not towards His face of whom in days of childhood
  Oft I had learnt beside my mother's knee
Did I look up when all the young man's wild blood
  Flashed through my veins and filled the heart of me.

Nay, but far off in proudly vaunted science,
  Nay, but aloof in fondly imaged art
Long did I stand in impotent defiance,
  Bidding the faith of innocence depart.

Truths of a God and of the mythic healing
   Brought to lost souls by some superior mind?
Lo they were fables of the priests' revealing,
   Fit for the superstitious of mankind.

Life was a sham, a falsehood, and a lying,
   Shifting its scenes and changing day by day,
Passing all swiftly till the time of dying
   Brought endless sleep to keep an endless sway.

Live it I would, but was that worth the living
   Which to the sight could show no prospect clear?
Live it I would although no power of giving
   Did it possess of things that make life dear.

So wrapped in thoughts that sprang from the reliance
   On the young heart made hot by human pride,
Gave I to God and to his faith defiance,
   Scorning the Saviour and the Man who died!

III.

Tell me no tale of God, O man who straineth
  After his truth until your mind is weak.
Look out on earth and tell me what he gaineth
  Who strives to mount yon barren hill-side
    peak?

If there be God, what make you of your learning?
  If there be God, which God is he you teach?
Who is the God evolved from your discerning,
  What is the truth embodied in your speech?

Nay, but no man will give your speech his credit
  In the diversity that meets each sun.
Even the Christ you preach to-day hath said it—
  'There is one sheep-fold and the sheep are
    one.'

Say, are ye one? Nay, surely, but with smiling,
  Surely with scorn not more than ye deserve,
Have I looked forth and heard the fierce reviling
  Of man with man in His name whom ye serve!

IV.

Once on this earth, it tells in holy writing,
  Walked there a Man who more than men was great;
Who in the works of love took strange delighting
  From earliest sunbeam till the night waxed late.

Yea, and of Him, that wondrous Galilean,
  Rings the wide world with no scant song of praise!
Yea, and of Him shall man upraise strong paean,
  Until the ending of the world's last days.

Yea, but if He could look from forth His sadness,
  Back from the green hills where His tired feet trod,

How would He see the blindness and the
    madness
  Shown in the minds of them that call Him
    God?

Wondrous example of the highest highest!
Prophet or preacher, in Whose mind I hail
Something akin, and coming near the nighest
  Unto that perfectness which now is pale:

Framer of laws of love and of forgiving,
  How have they mocked Thee who Thy name
    revere!
How have they framed their lives upon Thy
    living,
  How have they held the truths that Thou
    heldst dear?

Lo where the fire glows ghastly in the city,
  Lo where the stake uprears its murd'rous
    head,
Taking no heed of Christ's o'ershadowing pity,
  Mindful in nothing of the tears he shed!

V.

So in the place of Him Whom my soul scorning
   Held far aloof from and believed no word,
Made I myself dear gods of springtime morning,
   Bursting of flower, and song of hedgeside bird.

O'er English fields by rising sun just lighted
   Oft strayed my feet and brushed the early dew :
All that was best within me much delighted
   With what I saw and recognised as true.

Or in a noontide in some upland meadow
  Stretched by the brook that murmered on
      its way
Forth from its shelter in the mountain's shadow,
  Reading the clouds that floated by, I lay.

Yes, and it seemed that nature's face was
      dearer,
  Dearer and fairer than the face of God.
Yes, and it seemed that nature brought me
      nearer
  Unto that path which minds of reason trod.

VI.

Then from the lap of nature home returning
    What time the sun sank down beyond the sea,
Trimmed I my lamp and underneath its burning
    Pored o'er the wealth of love and mystery;

Lingered till late o'er poet's old-time rhyming,
    Rapt in its lore while twilight hours went by
And the stars rose, and lo, the white moon climbing
    Over the cloud hills of the midnight sky!

Pored I o'er page of philosophic meaning,
    Reading the words of men who dared to think,
Tremblingly strove to gather up a gleaning
    Out of their fields and at their well to drink.

Yea, and I thought, and full well do I know it,
　That more in book and scroll of wondrous eld,
That more in writ of seer and of poet
　Is the true faith and greater creed beheld.

In the ideal found I truest glory,
　Building a principle of fancied worth
Greater by far than aught of priestly story,
　Wiser by far than aught of fabled birth.

And in the glass of dread mysterious science
　Marked I the world of pre-historic man;
Watched the machines of nature's great appliance
　Saw the evolving of her wondrous plan.

Yea, so I learned, until the last faint presence
　Of dying faith died out and was not seen;
Yea, and I cried in that weird evanescence
　God there is none, nor hath there ever been!

VII.

And in the fierce dissension round me raging
  Cherished and fostered in the name of Christ,
Saw I strong proof that old-time faiths were aging,
  Felt that a man no more might be enticed

Out of that path of science and of reason
  Which when once trod shall make his manhood free,
Secure at all points from the taint of treason;
  Strong in a faith from which old faiths should flee.

And from afar as the enthusiast gazes
   O'er burning sands to Mecca's destined walls
Did I look forth to where the free sun blazes
   Over the free land where no shadow falls.

Lo and I cried— Behold the time draws nigher,
   Lo I have seen the opening of that way
Wherein man climbs towards a vastly higher
   Faith than the faith ye blindly preach to-day!

VIII.

But the long years passed on and found me restless,
   Rising at morn in search of some new faith,
Seeking all day as seeks a tired bird nestless
   After a home and finding but a wraith.

Ever I cried in bitter aspiration,
   Give me but rest in science or in art,
Let me but know the mutual inspiration
   Of some communing with another heart.

Ay, for despite the proud and stern denial
   Of God and faith there still remained a trace
Of Him Whose life was spent in bitter trial,
   Some faint remembrance of His thorn-crowned face.

Yea, in the wisdom of that evolution
   With which I strove to make all nature pure
Some sense of mine made inner revolution
   And cried Thou guessest, but the truth is sure!

IX.

Also at last there came a fearful doubting,
   Mixed with strange phantoms of some devil bred,
Ghastly and grim and drear with ghostly shouting,
   Making weird mocking of the words I said.

So did they pluck my very soul asunder
   Torn from this side to that with fevered mind,
Swayed for one second with imagined wonder,
   Dashed to the earth and as the blindest, blind.

Ay and the soul within me made its plaining,
   Crying for aid against my sin's control;
Calling, O help, thou help of the complaining,
   Praying, O aid, thou aid of every soul.

Yea, but the light came not upon the morrow;
   Nay, for the light came not for many days.
Through diverse paths of human love and sorrow
   Did Thy Soul lead me to the peaceful ways.

X.

Arise O heart and fill thee with sweet
 madness,
 Wake thee O life and live thyself anew!
—Yea, for love's voice had charmed away the
 sadness
 Which once in silence and in dread I knew.

Even as far off the voyager who ventures
 Forth into unknown deeps and sees some
 isle
Glow through the darkness of his drear
 adventures,
 Lighting his pathway with enticing smile:

Even as of old in the Arthurian story
 The knight from far perceived a radiance pale,
And knew the glimmer of that perfect glory
 Circling and burning round the holy grail:

Even as the one who forth through fell and
 forest
 Perils dear life to track an unknown land,
Sees when some day his need is at its sorest
 Glad golden gleam of very furthest strand:

Even as one who o'er a fond invention
 Bends pale and thin with never word of cheer,
Suddenly sees through some chance intervention
 The project finished and the pathway clear:

So O beloved do I look upon thee!
 So O beloved do I see thee now,
Where the glad summer sunlight falling on thee
 Gilds into gold the blossoms at thy brow.

XI.

Arise O sun from out the eastern ocean,
  Arise and fill the sleeping land with light,
And touch to gold the waves' unceasing motion,
  O glad forerunner of a morning bright.

Rise and mount higher through the cloudless heaven,
  Soar on quick wings from point to point and fly
Fast on thy way until thy hand has given
  The June day forth and brought the June night nigh.

So with a grandeur and a shining splendour,
  Rise and go forth, O golden-vested sun,
Bringing that hour when twilight pale and tender
  Shall blend two spirits and two lives in one.

XII.

So through the noontide loveliness we wandered
   Where love made heaven beside the southern
      sea,
Or in the twilight spake no word, but pondered
   On love's enchantment and his mystery.

Oft did we watch the stars that in strange
      brightness
   Lighted the heavens beyond the inland hill,
Or saw the moon in pale etherial whiteness
   Witch the wild waves to silver at her will.

And though I marked the earth with beauty
      laden,
   Tracked the broad sky, and traced the forest
      life
Nothing I found so perfect as the maiden
   Proved and made dearer by the name of
      Wife!

XIII.

Take thou no thought, O heart, for any morrow;
   Live for to-day! So cried I ere the hand
Of unseen power had laid my soul in sorrow,
   And the sun set upon a darkened land.

And what is sorrow? Has a word defined it,
   Can subtle minds its secrets penetrate?
Nay, but the life wherein God's care hath shrined it
   Cry as it may must calmly watch and wait.

O sorrow that is human! in thy teaching
   Surely God speaketh and His voice is heard
Even as the voice of the Evangelist preaching
   The speedy advent of th' Incarnate Word.

God leads no soul by pleasant paths to heaven,
   Nor is it good that life should all be bright.
What! is the triumph of the warrior striven
   Less grand because he passed through fiercest fight?

Nay, surely. For in every acclamation,
  In every shouting of the throngèd square
That hails him darling of the conquering nation,
  In cheer of man and smile of woman fair,

In all he joys; but in the joying turns him
  Away to thinking of the tented field;
Once more the lust of blood consumes and
    burns him;
  Once more his arms are braced, his soul is
    steeled

To deeds of might; he hears once more the
    crying
  Of stricken men; the whistling bullets' storm
Whirl into life and die away in sighing
  Over cold hearts that once were beating
    warm.

So he remembers as they throng around him
  Bringing him home in triumph on his way;
So does he think the while their shouts
    surround him—
' All this I braved for my reward to-day!'

XIV.

And through all this my soul has come anear
    Him
    Whom once I scorned and now I trust so
    well
Let me then cry Behold Him and draw near Him
    He, He it was that raised me when I fell!

He is the Christ! Behold His bearing tender,
    Look on those eyes that long to pierce thy soul;
The very stars are less than He in splendour:
    The teeming ages round Him reverent roll.

His ways are not the ways of man: He knoweth
    Every temptation, and each snare He knows
And to the heart that blindly trusts He showeth
    The perfect way and guides it as it goes.

He is the Christ, the only one oblation,
    The God made man to Whom till time be past
There shall be drawn th' illimitable nation
    Of those that long to see His face at last.

PART FIVE.

He ends his life in a Monastery.

I.

Holy Saint Francis of the face benign!
   Here in thy cloister, whence the eye looks down
O'er vine clad fields upon the little town
Sleeping in sunlight that seems half-divine,
Ten years have passed above this head of mine,
   Ten years, sweet years, empty of sigh or frown,
   Yea, 'tis ten years—how quickly are they flown!

Sweet saint, thou knowest why—those eyes
    of thine
That look on me so calmly from thy place
    In highest heaven have seen my Lord and
    love.
Yea, thou, O holy saint, hast seen His face.
    Thou lookest on it now and so dost prove
How glorious and how perfect is the grace
    Of Him who died on earth and reigns above.

II.

See here in the Scriptorium, old and grey,
A missal which was not made yesterday,
Nor twenty years since, but has laid here long,
As in the poet's fancy hides a song.
How old it is! What thick rough edges too:
Here's good Saint Francis in a gown of blue,
And the Blest Virgin with the Holy Child.
See His round eyes and little face so mild.
Here's Herod with his robe and crown awry,
The grave Magicians standing calmly by,
And Saint Veronica beside the cross
With good Saint John weeping their Master's
    loss,
And Stephen, looking upward to the skies,
With claspèd hands and supplicating eyes;
And here the children round our Saviour's
    knees,—
Would that we, brother, were as pure as these!
Ah well, and let us read a little, too,
And see what he that made this missal, knew.
See, here is written on the opening leaf

*" Time is not long; the longest life is brief,
Ye that here read, as ye to Heaven would go,
Pray for the soul of Fra Angelico."*
Read, brother then: the page is open there.

"Long years ago, how long I cannot tell,
An angel from on high went down to Hell,
And asked of one that burnt there why he fell,

"To whom the burning soul in accents low,
Weeping hot tears the while he spake said 'Lo
Once sinful pride within my heart did glow

"'So fearfully that I was lifted high
In my own mind and fearèd no power, I,
Nor ever thought that God was standing by.

"'Nor owned Him Lord, but day by day
        waxed great
In mine own strength and made me desolate,
And in my heart kept stern and awful state.

"'And yet fell not because of this,—for He
Bears long and well sin 'gainst His Majesty,
And had forgiven at one slight word from me,—

"'But because I, in malice, once did lay
Dark snares to make a young heart fall away
Whose soul was white as are the buds of May.

"'And seeing this, on me God's anger burst,
'Who sins, said He, shall surely be accurst,
But he that tempts is counted e'er the worst.'"

"Then wept he once again and turned to flee
Back to his wilds of hopeless misery.
—O thou that readest, take this unto thee,

"And learn that any sin is washed away
Sooner than his that doth a soul betray
Because that soul is turned from its white way

"—Where it had wandered quietly and well—
Unto the path which leadeth on to Hell,
Wherein the devil and his angels dwell.

"O thou that readest, does thy memory know
Of any sin against a soul of snow?
God not forgets it if thou hast done so."

III.

Angelus sounds across the quiet meadows:
   Here let me kneel and intercession make,
Until around me fall the evening shadows,
   With her who loves us for her dear Son's sake.

Mother of God and Queen of highest heaven!
   Ah Mary hear us when we ask of Thee
To pray for us for whom thy Son has striven,
   For whom He died upon the blessèd Tree.

And hearing kneel in thy sweet solemn whiteness
   With all true saints before the Eternal Throne,
Ah pray for us and let us feel the lightness
   Of perfect peace and know our fault is gone.

Mary, thine eyes have looked upon Him dying,
   Thine arm hath held Him as a little child,
Ah bid Him look on us all-suppliant lying
   O blessèd one, O virgin undefiled.

Plead with Him, mother of the sheep that love
 Him,
  Kneel to Him, Lily of celestial fields!
Mary, thy love is round Him and above Him,
  And thou canst sway the sceptre which He
   wields.

Star of the Ocean! See while night comes
  stealing
  Over the hills that watch yon peaceful bay,
The bell that calls us to thy praise is pealing :
  Grant us to praise for ever and for aye.

Hail Mary! Hail Queen, Mother, Saint most
  Glorious!
  Kneeling in Heaven before thy Monarch
   Son,
Help us to come from out the fight victorious,
  Stretch forth thy hand to aid us when 'tis
   done!

IV.

After long years my heart is come anear Thee,
  Soon shall I reach Thee whom I love so well.
O Saviour Christ, what joy to see and hear Thee,
  O Holy Lord, how sweet Thy praise to tell!

Yea, death steals nigh me. Welcome, God's own angel,
  Welcome, blest shadow bearing sword or spear;
Thou art to me as is a sweet evangel,
  For thou to Him I love wilt bring me near.

ANIMA CHRISTI.

Dying, you say? Ah me, the news is glorious!
   Soon shall I see Him Who hath all my
      thought;
Yea, I shall come from out the fight victorious,
   Led by His hand Who my salvation bought.

How can I tell you what my heart is feeling,
   How can I speak of what my soul expects?
Listen—1 hear the angelic anthem pealing,
   —Or is't some song my fancy recollects?

Do they sing matins in the church below us,
   Is it the mass, or is it eventide?—
Nay, but in dying God doth often show us
   What doth await us at the other side.

Visions we have of those bright homes of glory,
   Glimpses of what for us is kept in store,
Visions surpassing poet's wildest story,
   Visions that steal through heaven's half-open
      door.

If I could tell you what doth there await me,
  If I could say what joy is there for me,
How ye would long through yon still vale to
    mate me,
  How ye would burn with zeal that sight to
    see!

    *   *   *   *   *

Will it not kill me, this fierce, fond, devotion?
  Will it not make me speechless where I
    stand?
Nay, for His love is boundless as the ocean,
  And He will clasp me with His strong right
    hand,

And bear me onward to the throne before Him,
  To kneel all humbly at the feet of God.
And then—but how shall I, a worm, adore Him?
  How shall I dare to wait His mighty nod?

ANIMA CHRISTI.

How shall I dare to look on God the Father?
—How did I dare to look on God the Son?
Yea, and the Son shall beg His mercy, rather
　Than that my soul should faint ere heaven be won.

Yea, he shall pray, shall plead in accents tender
　His death, till God the Father shrives my soul,
And bids me wait before Him in His splendour
　While the vast ages round Him reverent roll.

Yea, Christ the Saviour, Christ the One Oblation,
　Hath found me pardon and my time is past:
O let me go to join that mighty nation,
　O let me look upon His face at last!

V.

Can this be Death? Methinks your faces fade
And a strange darkness gathers round my bed
Only to be dispersed by light more strange.
Where are you O my friends that pray for me?
I hear your voices.—
     Nay, even they are gone,
And this is Death. The world is far behind,
And I have stepped into a narrow vale
Full of weird horror. It is the agony
Which every soul must pass through at such hour,
When every deed that ever life has known
Passes in swift review, and every sin
Is met once more in exquisite remorse.
Jesu, have mercy! Mary, pray for me!
Some angel from the Lord come unto me.
And yonder through the darkness comes a light
That grows into the figure of a man,
Or of an angelic messenger. O joy,
Surely it is the presence of the Lord
Who comes to welcome me! Into Thy hands,
O Lord, into Thy hands.—

VI.

Thus, wondrous Spirit, whom, seeing not, we know
  By faith not sight, Thou leadest, through strange ways
Unto the destined end! Be Thine the praise
That any soul is brought from endless woe,
From suffering, and the life which is below,
  Into the searching presence of the blaze
  Of Thy high Heaven. Here in this wordly maze
Where few friends are and mighty is the foe
We wander, looking upward to Thy heaven,
  Sinning and sinned against from day to day,
Soul-sick, mind-tossed, and sometimes from Thee driven
  Yet not by Thee permitted far to stray.
Ah, the blest joy, when we, from all sin shriven
  O Soul of Christ, shall be with Thee for aye!

THE END.

DEDICATION.

The evening lamp burns faint and low,
And in the corners of my room
There dwells an undefinèd gloom
Of shadows, and the flickering glow
Of the red fire is almost spent.
Let it die out. I am content:
The pages of my book are done.

To-night I saw the autumn sun
Sink slowly through the autumn sky.
A flock of birds went sailing by
And passed into the crimson west
And faded in the twilight dun;
And if they sailed for some far nest
I know not, but the thought arose
Within me that the poet knows

Nothing of where his wingèd thought
Shall fly nor where it shall be brought
By angel hands, nor who shall grasp
The truths he fain would teach, nor clasp
The faith he longs to give to all.

Thy picture hangs upon my wall,
O priest and prince of Holy Church!
The whitened hair, the eyes that search
With questioning look the heart and life,
That see the intellectual strife;
The furrowed brow that tells of care.
It hangs perpetually there
Until it almost seems to speak.

And in these days of doctrine weak
Thank God for ev'ry man whose faith
Is something better than a wraith,
Whose voice has no uncertain sound,
Whose feet are firm on battle ground
Who speaks from certainty, and sees
Far into other times than these.

Thanks for the witnessing to Christ!
—Indeed the times are waxing late,
The foe knocks loudly at the gate,
He cries ' the old faiths have sufficed :
Let in the newer.' Nay, but we
Trust still in God and we will walk
In the old paths and the old ways,
And even though unbelief shall stalk
Through all the land, and mockery
Should wait upon its steps we still
Will trust upon His holy will
Whose Presence is with us all days.

How shall I tell thee this is thine,
O preacher of the silver tongue,
Upon whose words my soul has hung
To drink the soul-sufficing wine
Of thy swift thought ? To thee I bring
This tale of one soul's wandering.

—But 'tis no time to day for songs,
To-day is time to think of wrongs
Needing redress and sympathy.
The land is wet with heavy tears.

And yet in the approaching years
—O happy years!—I seem to see
A day when all hearts shall be free
And life shall be one long glad rhyme;
When true equality shall reign,
And there shall not be any pain,
And every soul as snow be white.
For now are the last hours of night,
And lo! there comes the rising sun
To light the illimitable day
When all tears shall be wiped away,
And God shall mould all creeds in One!

WORKS BY THE SAME AUTHOR.

OPINIONS OF THE PRESS.

EARLY POEMS.

(1882).

"New phases of thought and feeling in language rich in poetic beauty, and in rhyme which lingers on the ear like a strain of music. Mr. Fletcher treats not only of nature in various aspects, but with a true poet's sympathy, gives us some fine lines on the death of Longfellow and on Wordsworth's birth-place."—*National Church.*

"Mr. Fletcher writes with taste and feeling, and there is true poetic fervour, as well as chaste expression, in his verses. *The Dusk of the Gods,* the closing poem in the book, is a fine piece of imaginative work. Something very different is *An Idyll.* The scene is laid in Cumberland, and the style is Wordsworthian, and good enough to be suggestive of the truest of the Lake poets."—*Leeds Mercury.*

OPINIONS OF THE PRESS.

"As first fruits they indicate not a little promise. The author has evidently studied well the great masters of song, especially Wordsworth; and has caught something of their spirit. He succeeds in touching some true poetic chords, and his verse is sweet and musical."—*Literary World.*

"*An Idyll*, describing a quiet Cumberland village, is especially sweet and breathes throughout the true spirit of poetry. The lyrics are especially beautiful and are written in the true Wordsworthian vein . . . all the fervour and originality of genius."—*Maryport Advertiser.*

"There are few persons who read the book who will not admit that it contains not only promise of the future, but much of positive merit. There is imagination in Mr. Fletcher's work and a facility in composition which removes him far out of the ordinary level of youthful writers of verse."—*Western Daily Press.*

ANIMA CHRISTI.
(1884).

"It is long since we met with a poem which has so completely engrossed us as *Anima Christi*. From the exquisite sonnet which serves as a prologue, down to the last line, the author shows himself as a true poet and a sound Christian philosopher. We do not quote, for the mere reason that it is impossible to select from the many beauties of the poem. Mr. Fletcher's verse may, for its melody, bear comparison with that of our best-known writers. We shall look to meet this author again."—*Graphic.*

" Mr. Fletcher's *Anima Christi* is a singularly impressive record of the struggles of a soul onward and upward, from the darkness and despair of Atheism to the brightness and comfort of Christian hope and faith. Sweet and solemn strains . . . it is a poetical idealisation not at all out of harmony with human experience." —*Literary World.*

" Of much great poetic merit is the volume before us. Mr. Fletcher writes intelligibly enough and has a good ear for rhythm. Moreover he has not only imagination but passion. Altogether Mr. Fletcher is a writer of promise."—*Derby Mercury.*

" In more than one respect this is a remarkable poem. The vast variety of thought, composition, and poetry contained in it bespeak genius of no common order. Throughout the whole we meet with a startling boldness of expression, and everywhere with instances of the tones of true inspiration."—*Hull News.*

OPINIONS OF THE PRESS.

"This is a poem of great merit, and has already secured for its author a considerable reputation in the literary world. Exquisite lyrics . . . the stanzas glow with some of the most beautiful thoughts we have ever met with."—*Bookseller.*

"*Anima Christi* has poetic merit and much genial emotion. The sonnet by which the poem is introduced is marked by dignity and truth. There are verses here and there full of sweetness."—*Tablet.*

"A remarkable book. The author possesses considerable merit, amounting almost to inspiration. The value and beauty of human love is shown in some passages of exquisite sweetness. We hope Mr. Fletcher will give us further evidence of his genius and devotion."—*Weekly Churchman.*

"A striking poem. The interest of the book is well sustained and passages here and there are of great poetical beauty."—*Publishers' Circular.*

"*Anima Christi* portrays the passage of a soul from the material assurance of Agnosticism into the bosom of the Church through the interposition of the *ewigweibliche* influence. Mr. Fletcher's conception is worthy of realization; and his work contains sufficient indications of the poetic faculty to make us hope he may attain to more adequate and perfect fulfilment of future conceptions."—*Saturday Review.*

OPINIONS OF THE PRESS.

"A new poet of an order much superior to many of those who have risen to some degree of poetic celebrity. Many original and happy turns of thought, many lines of real beauty, and many stanzas of unusual power."— *Baptist Magazine.*

"It . . . . . impresses one with its reality and earnestness, and in the latter part there are some fine and passionate stanzas. The whole may be commended to those who are in sympathy with the writer's sentiment."—*Guardian.*

"The lyrical passages in the second and third parts are of considerable merit. We are glad to find that another volume by the same author is to appear."—*Month.*

"Let me now thank you for a very striking poem."— H. E. CARDINAL NEWMAN.

DEUS HOMO.
(1887).

"Mr. Fletcher is an eloquent pleader; he feels very strongly, and his poems are an outcome of his feeling. Loving Truth and Justice above all things, above all loving the Supreme Truth, he overflows with sorrow and indignation at the denial of that Truth, and the perhaps still worse indifference displayed towards it by men: at the selfishness of the world, and its neglect for the poor—the 'Brothers of Christ.' His blank verse is excellent: we are sorry there is only one piece, *Fra Guiseppe's Sermon* in this metre. *Midnight in the Strand* is a touching little piece, and equally touching are the lines entitled *Real Presence*. We are sure Mr. Fletcher's book will find a responsive echo in every generous heart. For ourselves we gladly give it welcome."—*Month*.

"After a very energetic and telling preface on the necessity for more wide-spread thoroughness in religious faith Mr. Fletcher gives us in thoughtful and refined verse cogent argument of the Divinity of the God-Man... There are also in this little volume some touchingly pathetic and simple minor poems. The work is altogether most interesting and ennobling."—*West Kent Advertiser*.

"The preface is the proper entrance to a book, as the door into the pasture fold. In the case of the above poem, the vigorous and outspoken prose introduction should most certainly be read. The poem which follows is the outburst of a heart grieved and indignant, because God Incarnate has come to His own, and so many of His own receive Him not."—*Faith of our Fathers*.

OPINIONS OF THE PRESS.

"I have been very much impressed by the dignity and beauty of your poetry and rejoice to find so earnest and cultivated a man devoting himself so sincerely to a good cause. I remember being genuinely impressed by your *Anima Christi* but in some ways I prefer *Deus Homo*. It is a relief in these days of innumerable versifiers to encounter a real poet."—*William Sharp.*

"1 thank you for all the zeal and devotion which you evince in the good cause."—+Robert, *Bishop of Leeds.*

www.ingramcontent.com/pod-product-compliance
Lightning Source LLC
Chambersburg PA
CBHW031354160426
43196CB00007B/815